IMPORTANT MEISSEN

AND OTHER PORCELAINS

The Collection of a

NEW YORK LADY

STERLING SILVER TABLEWARE

Specially designed for

JOHN W. CAMPBELL

NEW YORK CITY

OBJECTS OF ART

SILK SHAWLS • FINE FRENCH FANS

From the Estate of

MARY G. CARROLL

NEW YORK CITY

With few additions

PUBLIC AUCTION SALE—April 8th at 2 P.M.
EXHIBITION—From April 4th until sale

AT THE

JAY GOULD MANSION
579 FIFTH AVENUE AT 47TH STREET

KENDE GALLERIES OF GIMBEL BROTHERS
NEW YORK
1944

NUMBER ONE HUNDRED FIFTY-THREE

IMPORTANT MEISSEN
AND OTHER PORCELAINS

The Collection of a

NEW YORK LADY

Sold by Her Order

STERLING SILVER TABLEWARE

Specially designed for

JOHN W. CAMPBELL
NEW YORK CITY

OBJECTS OF ART
JEWELRY • BIBELOTS
SILK SHAWLS • FINE FRENCH FANS

From the Estate of

MARY G. CARROLL
NEW YORK CITY

Sold by Order of
Senator Hiram Bingham
Executor

With few additions

PUBLIC AUCTION SALE—Saturday, April 8th at 2 P.M.
EXHIBITION—From Tuesday, April 4th until sale
(Daily 10 A.M.-6 P.M.)

Illustrated Catalogue 25c

AT THE

JAY GOULD MANSION
579 FIFTH AVENUE AT 47TH STREET

KENDE GALLERIES OF GIMBEL BROTHERS
NEW YORK
1944

CONDITIONS OF SALE

The property listed in this catalogue will be offered and sold subject to the following terms and conditions:

1. The word "Galleries," wherever used in these Conditions of Sale means the Kende Galleries, Inc.

2. The Galleries have exercised reasonable care to catalogue and describe correctly the property to be sold, but they do not warrant the correctness of description, genuineness, authenticity or condition of said property.

3. The Galleries reserve the right to withdraw any article from sale for any reason whatsoever before the article is offered for sale.

4. Unless otherwise announced by the auctioneer at the time of sale, all bids are to be for the lot as a whole and as numbered in the catalogue.

5. The highest bidder accepted by the auctioneer shall be the buyer. In the event of any dispute between bidders, the auctioneer may, in his discretion, determine who is the successful bidder, and his decision shall be final; or the auctioneer may reoffer and resell the article in dispute.

6. Any bid which is not commensurate with the value of the article offered, or which is merely a nominal or fractional advance over the previous bid, may be rejected by the auctioneer, in his discretion, if in his judgment such bid would be likely to affect the sale injuriously.

7. The name and address of the buyer of each article, or lot, shall be given to the Galleries immediately following the sale thereof, and payment of the whole purchase price, or such part thereof as the Galleries may require, shall be immediately made by the purchaser thereof. If the foregoing condition, or any other applicable condition herein, is not complied with, the sale may, at the option of the Galleries, be cancelled, and the article or lot, reoffered for sale.

8. Unless the sale is advertised and announced as an unrestricted sale, or a sale without reserve, consignors reserve the right to bid.

9. Except as herein otherwise provided, title will pass to the highest bidder upon the fall of the auctioneer's hammer, and thereafter the property is at the purchaser's sole risk and responsibility.

10. Articles sold and not paid for in full and not taken by noon of the third day following the sale may be turned over by the Galleries to a carrier to be delivered to a storehouse for the account and risk of the purchaser, and at his cost. If the purchase price has not been so paid in full, the Galleries may either cancel the sale, and

any partial payment already made shall be returned by the Galleries as liquidated damages, or they may resell the same without notice to the buyer and for his account and risk, and hold him responsible for any deficiency.

11. Property purchased will be delivered only on presentation of a receipted bill. The Galleries reserve the right to make delivery to any person presenting such receipted bill. If a receipted bill is lost before delivery, the buyer should immediately notify the Galleries.

12. If for any cause whatsoever any article sold cannot be delivered or cannot be delivered in as good condition as the same may have been at the time of sale, the sale will be cancelled without any liability to the Galleries and any amount that may have been paid on account of the sale will be returned to the purchaser.

13. In addition to the purchase price, the buyer will be required to pay any Federal, State and local taxes now or hereafter imposed upon the sale of the article or articles, unless the buyer is exempt from the payment thereof.

14. The Galleries, subject to these Conditions of Sale and to such terms and conditions as they may prescribe, but without charge for their services, will undertake to make bids for responsible parties approved by them. Requests for such bidding must be given with such clearness as to leave no room for misunderstanding as to the amount to be bid and must state the catalogue number of the item and the name or title of the article to be bid on. The Galleries reserve the right to decline to undertake to make such bids.

15. The records of the Galleries are in all cases to be considered final.

16. The Galleries will facilitate the employment of carriers and packers by purchasers, but will not be responsible for the acts of such carriers or packers in any respect whatsoever.

17. These Conditions of Sale cannot be altered except in writing by the Galleries or by public announcement by the auctioneer at the time of sale.

SALES CONDUCTED BY A. N. BADE AND L. A. CRACO

KENDE GALLERIES AT GIMBEL BROTHERS

33RD STREET & BROADWAY · NEW YORK

11th Floor

Telephone PEnnsylvania 6-5185   *Cable* KENDARTGAL

SATURDAY, APRIL 8TH, 1944, AT 2 P.M.

CATALOGUE NUMBERS 1 TO 214, INCLUSIVE

FINE FRENCH FANS AND SHAWLS

1. TWO PAINTED AND DECORATED FANS
   EARLY XIX CENTURY
   Painted with mythological scenes on paper, on pierced and gilt mother-of-pearl staves in rocailles, flowers and scroll ornament design; the other, ivory staves pierced in geometrical design. (imperfect). (*Carroll*).

2. THREE DECORATED FANS
   One Chinese with carved tortoise shell staves having black muslin fan with spangles; another with black lace on red lacquer staves, and a third, a paper fan with ornamental painted design. (*Carroll*).

3. THREE PAINTED AND DECORATED FANS
   Painted silk fan with mythological scene and grapevine on mother-of-pearl staves, circa 1820; another, with figural scenes printed on paper on gilt wooden staves and a third, Chinese metal gilt, pierced and enameled fan. (imperfect). (*Carroll*).

4. COLLECTION OF FANS
   Of various periods, makes and designs. (all imperfect). (7 pieces). (*Carroll*).

5. THREE FANS
   A green silk fan embroidered with spangles on pierced and gilt *ecailles blonde* staves, circa 1820; a black tulle fan embroidered with spangles on tortoise shell staves, and a third, black tulle fan embroidered with spangles on carved ebony staves. (*Carroll*).

6. FOUR PAINTED AND DECORATED FANS
   Painted on glaze with flowers, birds and figural scenes, three having ivory, and one, mother-of-pearl staves. (imperfect). (*Carroll*).

7. FOUR PAINTED FANS
   Three painted on glaze with flowers, having ivory staves; one, with painted peacock on paper having wooden staves. (imperfect). (*Carroll*).

5

8. FOUR IVORY FANS

Two pierced, one with ornamental design painted with landscapes and flowers, the other Chinese. Also, two plain ivory fans, monogrammed. (*Carroll*).

9. TWO FRENCH GILDED AND SILVERED MOTHER-OF-PEARL AND DECORATED FANS

Staves pierced and gilded in floral designs with foils decorated with figures in period costumes flanked by floral designs in colors. (one stave in need of repair). (*New Jersey Private Collector*).

10. TWO FRENCH GILDED AND SILVERED IVORY AND DECORATED FANS

One with pierced staves in floral design with foils depicting three women with swans; the other, having staves pierced and gilded in floral and geometrical designs centering figural scene. Foils decorated with printed figural scenes and floral designs in colors. (*New Jersey Private Collector*).

11. TWO LOUIS PHILLIPE FINELY CARVED IVORY AND DECORATED FANS   *Circa* 1840

Staves elaborately carved in floral designs and gilded, silvered and copper flowers in relief. Foils decorated with figural scenes in landscape background. (one stave in need of repair). (*New Jersey Private Collector*).

12. THREE FRENCH IVORY AND DECORATED FANS

One with staves depicting figural scene and foils having similar scene in cartouche and floral and scroll design in gold sequins; another, with staves pierced and decorated with flowers in colors with foils having shepherd scene in cartouche on silver ground and the last, with pierced floral design silvered, and foils with figural scene in cartouche, surrounded by gilded floral and scroll designs. (*New Jersey Private Collector*).

13. LOUIS PHILLIPE GILDED AND SILVERED MOTHER-OF-PEARL AND DECORATED FAN   *Circa* 1840

Staves with silvered and gilded floral designs and having landscapes in colors in gold rimmed cartouches. The foils depicting dancing couples in landscape background. (*New Jersey Private Collector*).

14. LOUIS PHILLIPE GILDED AND SILVERED MOTHER-OF-PEARL AND DECORATED FAN   *Circa* 1840

Elaborately pierced staves of mother-of-pearl, gilded and silvered centering figural scene, the foils decorated with colored print depicting ladies and gentlemen in period costume. (*New Jersey Private Collector*).

6

15

15. FRENCH GILDED AND SILVERED MOTHER-OF-PEARL
AND PAINTED FAN
Jeanne Elisabeth Bouguereau, American: 1851-1922
Landscape scene with a peasant girl, at center, reclining on the edge
of a well holding a waterpot; on the reverse, well surrounded by
foliage. Painted on chicken skin and signed on the front, J. E.
BOUGUEREAU. Mounted on pierced mother-of-pearl staves with en-
graved floral decoration. (*Carroll*). [SEE ILLUSTRATION].
NOTE: Jeanne Elisabeth Bouguereau nee Gardner, was the wife and
pupil of Willem Adolphe Bouguereau, the famous French painter.

16. THREE FRENCH GILDED AND SILVERED IVORY AND
DECORATED FANS   *Circa* 1840
All with elaborately pierced and gilded staves in floral design with
foils depicting figural scenes and flowers in colors. (*New Jersey
Private Collector*).

17. TWO FRENCH DECORATED FANS
One with ivory staves pierced and decorated with floral garlands in
colors and having foils decorated with figures and landscape in cartouches and floral designs enlivened by colored sequins. The other,
with staves of mother-of-pearl pierced and gilded in floral design.
Foils having figural and landscape motifs. (*New Jersey Private
Collector*).

7

18. TWO FRENCH GILDED MOTHER-OF-PEARL AND
DECORATED FANS
One with elaborately pierced staves in gilded floral, leaf and urn
design and with foils depicting a court scene; the other, with pierced
staves in floral and festoon design one stave having figure of *putti*.
Foils depicting singer entertaining a group of listeners. (*New Jersey
Private Collector*).

19. LOUIS PHILLIPE GILDED AND BLANC-DE-CHINE
TORTOISE SHELL FAN   *Circa* 1840
Staves of pierced and gilded *blanc-de-Chine* in floral design and foils
printed in figural scenes and harvest designs in gold. (*New Jersey
Private Collector*).

20. TWO PAISLEY SHAWLS
One with allover multicolored stylized floral design on red ground;
the other of similar pattern with white star center. (*Carroll*).

21. A PAISLEY SHAWL AND TWO PLAIN WOOL SHAWLS
Paisley shawl with flower emblems on orange ground. (*Carroll*).

22. TWO PAISLEY SHAWLS AND A PLAID VELVET SCARF
(*Carroll*).

23. TWO SPANISH SILK SHAWLS
One turquoise; the other of rose pink, with long fringes. (*Carroll*).

STERLING SILVER AND SILVER PLATED WARE

Ivories, Jewelry and Bibelots

24. TWO IVORY CARVINGS
Standing *putti* as fiddler and cymbal player. On circular stepped
ebony base. (*New York Private Collector*).—*Height, 5½ inches.*

25. TWO IVORY CARVINGS
One, the Swiss Lion with inscription: "Helvetiorum fidei ac virtuti."
The other a girl holding up her skirt with left hand and carrying a
badminton racquet in her right hand. On stepped circular base. (*New
York Private Collector*).—*Height of figure, 4¾ inches; Length of
lion, 4½ inches.*

26. IVORY CARVING
A richly dressed woman with fans in each hand, standing in front
of a gate; on oval base. (*New York Private Collector*).—*Height, 4
inches.*

8

27. TORTOISE SHELL AND MOTHER-OF-PEARL CARD
CASE
Mother-of-pearl panels on either side bordered by bands of tortoise
shell. Hinged top. (*New York Private Collector*).

28. AMETHYST AND GOLD BROOCH AND EARRINGS
Brooch set with oval and earrings set with pear-shaped amethysts;
18 kt. gold rope and flower setting. (*New York Private Collector*).

29. CORAL AND GOLD BROOCH AND EARRINGS
Cluster of round coral beads of various sizes on 18 kt. gold mountings. (*New York Private Collector*).

30. CORAL AND GOLD BROOCH AND EARRINGS
Oval-shaped clusters of coral beads of various sizes on 18 kt. gold
mountings. (*New York Private Collector*).

31. GOLD AND AGATE BRACELET
Large oval agate in rope design, gold and enamel frame cen-
tered between two smaller agates on 18 kt. gold band. (*New York
Private Collector*).

32. COPPER ENAMEL VASE
Heart-shaped miniature vase decorated with *puttis* and flowers. (imperfect). (*New York Private Collector*).—*Height, 3⅛ inches.*

33. ECAILLE BLONDE AND GOLD SNUFFBOX WITH
MINIATURE   *Pierre Adolph Hall, Swedish: 1739-1793*
Circular box with finely ciselé gold mountings at edges, set with oval
portrait miniature at lid, depicting gentlemen with lightly powdered
hair, wearing a black coat and white jabot. Signed, HALL. (*New
York Private Collector*).—*Diameter, 2⅜ inches.*

34. BRONZE AND ENAMEL MINIATURE CLOCK
Quadrangular clock case with high domed cover supported by four
twisted columns, surmounted by figures of elephants; on square
base with angel-head feet. Allover enameled with figural scenes and
heads of women in medallions and scroll ornaments. (*New York
Private Collector*).—*Height, 5⅛ inches.*

35. SILVER ENAMELED SMALL TRAY
Oblong with rounded corners, enameled on interior with figural
scene and landscape on exterior. (*New York Private Collector*).—
Length, 4⅝ inches.

9

17 50 36. SILVER SNUFF BOX AND THREE IVORY PAPER
KNIVES
Indian silver egg-shaped box with hinged top, repousse with stylized
flowers. Ivory paper knives carved with lilies of the valley, leaves
and flowers. (*Carroll*).

37 50 37. SIX STEEL SCISSORS
Of various sizes. (*Carroll*).

6 38. FOUR SILVER PLATED OBJECTS
Covered sugar bowl, creamer, waste bowl and spoonholder, having
beaded edge and engraved floral decoration. (*New York Private
Collector*).

12 39. TWO SILVER PLATED BREAD BASKETS
One, footed circular with molded edge, upright loop handle, pierced
in geometrical design. The other, octagonal with reeded edge.—
Diameter, 10⅛ inches; length, 11½ inches.

20 40. SILVER PLATED COVERED ENTREE DISH
Oval with reeded edge, having two compartments. Domed cover,
loop handles.—*Length, 11½ inches.*

27 30 41. STERLING SILVER FRUIT BOWL
Deep foliated bowl with reeded edge and ribbed sides. Weight approximately 10 ounces.—*Diameter, 10 inches.*

55 42. TWELVE STERLING SILVER BOUILLON CUPS
Bell-shaped cup with loop handles on circular foot. Monogrammed.
Weight approximately 31 ounces. (*New York Private Collector*).

12 43. STERLING SILVER FLOWER VASE
Tapering octagonal vase with overlapping scalloped edge, domed
circular base. Weight approximately 12 ounces. (*New York Private
Collector*).—*Height, 13¾ inches.*

130 44. STERLING SILVER COFFEE SET
Comprising coffee pot, creamer, sugar bowl and tray. Paneled pear-
shaped coffee pot with long curved spout, loop handle and hinged
tapering cover; helmet-shaped creamer, semi-globular paneled sugar
bowl, on oblong tray with molded edge. All engraved with flowers
and medallions. Monogrammed. Weight approximately 48 ounces.

24 45. STERLING SILVER BOTTLE HOLDER
Bottle-shaped with loop handle, the whole pierced in lattice and
geometrical pattern. Weight approximately 15 ounces.—*Height, 10⅛
inches.*

10

46 PAIR STERLING SILVER CANDLESTICKS
Tapering octagonal shaft, drip cup and base. Monogrammed.
Weighted.—*Height, 8½ inches.*

47. TWELVE STERLING SILVER OBJECTS
Six brandy cups, bell-shaped on tall shaft and circular base, monogrammed; pair pepper shakers, urn-shaped on square base; two
hexagonal salts and one spoon; hexagonal napkin ring, monogrammed. Weight approximately 12 ounces. (one brandy cup dam-
aged).

48. PAIR STERLING SILVER CANDLESTICKS
Cylindrical shaft and candleholder, circular drip cup and domed
circular base. Weighted.—*Height, 5 inches.*

49. SIX STERLING SILVER ICE CREAM CUPS
Circular deep cup on cone-shaped foot, pierced with geometrical
pattern. Glass inset with floral etching. Weight approximately 6
ounces.

50. PAIR STERLING SILVER CANDLESTICKS
Cylindrical shaft with circular drip cups on circular base. Engraved
with floral and scroll design. Monogrammed. (*New York Private
Collector*).—*Height, 5 inches.*

51. EARLY VICTORIAN SILVER TRAY
Circular with undulated edge, elaborately wrought with shell and
rocaille ornaments and flowers. Similar ornaments engraved at center.
On curved and chased feet with shell and floral design. Weight approximately 52 ounces. (*New York Private Collector*).—*Diameter,
18¾ inches.*

THE COLLECTION OF STERLING SILVER TABLE-
WARE OF MR. JOHN W. AND MRS. ROSALIND
D. CAMPBELL

Each piece inscribed and dated under foot, "Designed and hand-
wrought for John W. Campbell." Hand wrought at the Kalo Shop,
Chicago and New York. All pieces with appliqued initial "C" at
border.

52. FLATWARE SET
Comprising twelve of each: dinner, luncheon, grapefruit, bouillon,
iced tea, dessert, tea, demi-tasse, salt spoons. Twelve of each: dinner,
fish, oyster, luncheon, salad forks. Twelve of each: dinner, luncheon,
fish, butter knives. Twelve cornholders, seventeen various serving
utensils, three piece carving set. (248 pieces). Weight approximately
345 ounces.

11

53

53. TEA AND COFFEE SET ON TRAY

Comprising hot water kettle on stand, coffee pot, teapot, milk pitcher, creamer, sugar bowl, tongs and tray. Slightly incurved paneled body, quadrangular spouts and handles, hinged tops with ivory finials. On oblong tray with foliated border. Weight approximately 290 ounces. [SEE ILLUSTRATION].

54. COFFEE SET ON TRAY

Comprising coffee pot, creamer, milk pitcher, sugar bowl, tongs and tray. Slightly incurved cylindrical body with panels, quadrangular handles and spouts, hinged tops with ivory finials. Circular rimmed tray. Weight approximately 61 ounces.

55. OVAL VEGETABLE DISH

Oval bowl with overlapping molded edge on incurved molded foot. Weight approximately 25 ounces (scratched).—*Length, 12½ inches.*

56. CIRCULAR VEGETABLE DISH

With foliated rimmed border. Weight approximately 19 ounces.—*Diameter, 12 inches.*

57. OVAL VEGETABLE DISH

Quatrefoil with overlapping molded edge on incurved oval **foot.** Weight approximately 15 ounces.—*Length, 10¼ inches.*

12

58
Top 59

58. FIVE-PART CHAFING DISH
Circular covered pan with ebony handle, fitted in circular two-handled dish on tripod handled stand, with spirit burner. Weight approximately 127 ounces. [SEE ILLUSTRATION].—*Diameter of pan,* 10⅓ *inches.*

59. LARGE COVERED PLATTER
Oval foliated rimmed platter with domed cover with loop handle. Weight approximately 93 ounces. [SEE ILLUSTRATION].—*Length,* 34¾ *inches.*

13

60. COVERED PLATTER

Similar to the preceding. Weight approximately 45 ounces. [SEE ILLUSTRATION ON OPPOSITE PAGE].—*Length, 15½ inches.*

61. PAIR COVERED PLATTERS

Similar to the preceding. Weight approximately 48 ounces.—*Length, 11⅜ inches.*

62. OVAL PLATTER

With shaped edge and foliated border. Weight approximately 18 ounces. (scratched).—*Length, 13¾ inches.*

63. OVAL PLATTER

Similar to the preceding. Weight approximately 29 ounces. (scratched).—*Length, 16⅞ inches.*

64. OVAL PLATTER

Similar to the preceding. Weight approximately 41 ounces. (scratched).—*Length, 22½ inches.*

65. OVAL PLATTER

Similar to the preceding. Weight approximately 71 ounces. (scratched).—*Length, 24½ inches.*

66. LARGE TRAY

Oblong tray with rounded corners. Weight approximately 83 ounces. —*Length, 20 inches.*

67. COVERED MUFFIN DISH

Semi-globular pierced cover with loop handle on a circular plate with foliated border. Weight approximately 26 ounces.—*Diameter, 9½ inches.*

68. TWELVE FINGER BOWLS

Deep bowls with overlapping foliated edge; glass liners. Weight approximately 49 ounces.—*Diameter, 4⅝ inches.*

69. TWELVE BUTTER CHIPS

Circular with foliated edge. Weight approximately 16 ounces.— *Diameter, 3 inches.*

70. SIX PEPPER SHAKERS

Trefoil pear-shaped. Weight approximately 7 ounces.—*Height, 2½ inches.*

71. SIX PEPPER SHAKERS

Similar to the preceding. Weight approximately 7 ounces.—*Height, 2½ inches.*

14

72. ICE BOWL WITH TONGS
Deep circular footed bowl with upright loop handles having pierced detachable inset with large tongs. Weight approximately 54 ounces. [SEE ILLUSTRATION].—*Diameter, 9¼ inches.*

73. LARGE CIRCULAR TRAY
With foliated border and rim. Weight approximately 26 ounces.— [SEE ILLUSTRATION].—*Diameter, 13 inches.*

74. SOUFFLE DISH
Semi-globular paneled bowl on ball feet with detachable edge. Having covered Pyrex ware inset. Weight approximately 25 ounces. [SEE ILLUSTRATION].—*Diameter, 9 inches.*

75. SOUFFLE DISH
Similar to the preceding. Weight approximately 25 ounces.— *Diameter, 9 inches.*

15

76. LARGE FRUIT BOWL
Hexafoil with flaring undulated edge on domed paneled foot. Weight approximately 35 ounces. [SEE ILLUSTRATION ON PRECEDING PAGE].—Diameter, 12¼ inches.

77. SAUCE BOAT AND LADLE
Oval with loop handle and paneled sides on quatrefoil tray. Weight approximately 18 ounces. [SEE ILLUSTRATION ON PRECEDING PAGE].—Length, 8¾ inches.

78. TWELVE NUT DISHES
Deep foliated bowls, trefoil with molded edge. Weight approximately 13 ounces.—Diameter, 2¼ inches.

79. CRUMB KNIFE WITH TRAY AND NAPKIN RING
Semi-circular tray and matching knife with foliated edge; also an oval napkin ring. Weight approximately 10 ounces.

80. PAIR VEGETABLE DISHES
Deep quatrefoil dish with molding at edge, on oval incurved foot. Weight approximately 29 ounces. (scratched).—Length, 10 inches.

81. WATER PITCHER
Ribbed ovoid with wide spout and square loop handle. Weight approximately 29 ounces.

82. WATER PITCHER
Similar to the preceding. Weight approximately 16 ounces.—Height, 8¼ inches.

83. SAUCE BOWL, CANDY DISH AND TRAY
Hexafoil deep footed sauce bowl with undulated edge, together with ladle; trefoil bell-shaped candy dish on curved tripart feet and a trefoil plate. Weight approximately 21 ounces.—Diameters from 4¾ to 6½ inches.

84. TWELVE SERVICE PLATES
Plain rimmed plate repousse with flower emblems at border, representing the flower of each of the twelve months. Weight 213 ounces. Diameter, 10¾ inches.

85. TWELVE BREAD AND BUTTER PLATES
Plain circular plate. Weight approximately 57 ounces.—Diameter, 6⅛ inches.

86. LARGE COMPOTE
Shallow hexafoil bowl with rimmed undulated edge on tapering cylindrical shaft with repousse petals at circular base. Weight approximately 41 ounces.—Diameter, 13 inches.

87. PAIR COMPOTES
Similar to the preceding. Weight approximately 12 ounces.—
Diameter, 5⅜ inches.

88. PAIR COMPOTES
Similar to the preceding. Weight approximately 20 ounces.—
Diameter, 6¾ inches.

89. COMPOTE
Similar to the preceding. Weight approximately 21 ounces.—
Diameter, 9¾ inches.

90. BUTTER DISH, MUSTARD POT AND JELLY JAR
Butter dish with foliated rimmed edge, pierced detachable inset;
mustard pot incurved cylindrical with paneled sides, domed hinged
cover and ladle; similar jelly jar without cover. Weight approximately 20 ounces.

91. DINNER BELL AND TWO SMALL PLATES
Bell with pierced handle and two trefoil plates. Weight approximately
7 ounces.

92. PAIR SMALL TRAYS
Oval with foliated border and rim. Weight approximately 19 ounces.
—*Length, 10 inches.*

93. PAIR CANDY DISHES
Trefoil on ball feet. Weight approximately 10 ounces.—*Diameter, 6
inches.*

94. FLOWER VASE
Slender ovoid with hexafoil flaring lip and flaring base. Weight
approximately 12 ounces.—*Height, 12½ inches.*

95. FLOWER VASE
Tapering cylindrical base with hexafoil overlapping mouth. Weight
approximately 25 ounces.—*Height, 7½ inches.*

97. SIX CANDLESTICKS
Globular candleholder supported by baluster shaft on circular base.
Weight approximately 38 ounces.—*Height, 7⅛ inches.*

17

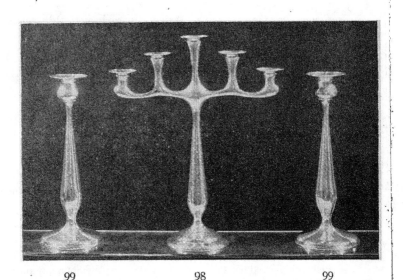

99   98   99

98. PAIR FIVE LIGHT GIRANDOLES

Baluster shaft on circular stepped base supporting two straight arms fitted with five graduated, tapering, cylindrical candleholders. Weight approximately 78 ounces. [SEE ILLUSTRATION].—*Height, 20 inches.*

99. PAIR TALL CANDLESTICKS

Globular candleholder with trefoil circular drip cup on paneled baluster shaft emanating from circular base with repousse petals. Weight approximately 47 ounces. [SEE ILLUSTRATION].—*Height,* 16 *inches.*

99A. PAIR TALL CANDLESTICKS

Similar to the preceding. Weight approximately 47 ounces.—*Height,* 16 *inches.*

100. PAIR BOOK ENDS AND A TRAY

Plain book ends with carved and pierced teakwood applique and an. oblong tray with curved sides. Weight approximately 32 ounces.— *Lengths,* 5½ *and* 12¼ *inches.*

18

XVIII AND XIX CENTURY EUROPEAN PORCELAINS

*Meissen, Nymphenburg, Frankenthal, Hoechst, Vienna,
Zurich, Berlin, Capo di Monte, Copenhagen.*

101. MEISSEN DECORATED PORCELAIN FIGURE
XIX CENTURY

Amor seated on clouds with green drapery over his knees; a heart on a cloud beside him; on a triangular base with inscription: "Je les accouple." (chipped). (*Property of a New York Lady*).—*Height, 5¼ inches.*

102. MEISSEN DECORATED PORCELAIN FIGURE
XIX CENTURY

A lady with lace-trimmed hoop skirt seated before a piano. On an oblong base with gilded decoration. (*Property of a New York Lady*).—*Height, 4¾ inches.*

103. MEISSEN DECORATED PORCELAIN FIGURE
XIX CENTURY

Amor, saluting, with quiver and scarf around body, on rocaille base. (imperfect). (*Property of a New York Lady*).—*Height, 6 inches.*

104. MEISSEN DECORATED PORCELAIN FIGURE
XIX CENTURY

Apollo seated on clouds, with rose drapery over his knees; he holds a lyre which rests on his knee in his right hand. (chipped). (*Property of a New York Lady*). [SEE ILLUSTRATION ON PAGE 31].—*Height, 11¼ inches.*

105. MEISSEN DECORATED PORCELAIN FIGURE
XIX CENTURY

Putto representing Summer; holding a sheaf of wheat in his right hand, having a green scarf tied around his shoulder, leaning against tree trunk. On irregular base with molded flowers. (imperfect). (*Property of a New York Lady*).—*Height, 5½ inches.*

106. MEISSEN DECORATED PORCELAIN FIGURE
XIX CENTURY

Putto representing Summer leaning against a tree trunk, with blue scarf around his back, holding a sheaf of wheat in his left arm, on irregular base. (imperfect). (*Property of a New York Lady*).—*Height, 5⅛ inches.*

19

107. TWO MEISSEN DECORATED PORCELAIN FIGURES

XVIII AND XIX CENTURY

One representing Winter; naked bearded man holding fur-lined wrap over his head and shoulders, leaning against a tree trunk; on rocaille base, circa 1780. The other *putto* as a fiddler wearing furred cap and pink scarf, on rocaille base. (both imperfect). (*Property of a New York Lady*).—*Heights, 3¾ and 5½ inches.*

108. MEISSEN DECORATED PORCELAIN FIGURE

XIX CENTURY

Standing figure of Amor with quiver hung around his shoulder and yellow scarf tied around body, leaning against a tree trunk; on triangular base, with inscription: "Je les balance." (imperfect). (*Property of a New York Lady*).—*Height, 5½ inches.*

109. MEISSEN DECORATED PORCELAIN FIGURE

XIX CENTURY

Figure of Amor making a face and scratching his head, with an empty quiver around shoulder and bow at his feet, leaning against tree trunk. On circular marbleized base. (*Property of a New York Lady*). (chipped). [SEE ILLUSTRATION ON OPPOSITE PAGE].—*Height, 7¾ inches.*

110. MEISSEN DECORATED PORCELAIN FIGURE

XIX CENTURY

Figure of Amor disguised as a Lady, wearing short striped underskirt and blue dress with train, and a bonnet; he holds a fan in his right hand and a scarf in his left hand. On circular marbleized base. (*Property of a New York Lady*). [SEE ILLUSTRATION ON OPPOSITE PAGE].—*Height, 9 inches.*

111. MEISSEN DECORATED PORCELAIN FIGURE

XIX CENTURY

Figure of Amor as a beggar with a wooden leg. Wearing torn blue frock and green trousers, holding his hat in his outstretched hand. He walks on crutches. On circular marbleized base. (*Property of a New York Lady*). [SEE ILLUSTRATION ON OPPOSITE PAGE].—*Height, 9 inches.*

112. MEISSEN DECORATED PORCELAIN FIGURE

XIX CENTURY

Figure of Amor breaking a heart, with quiver around shoulder, leaning against a tree trunk. On circular marbleized base. (*Property of a New York Lady*). [SEE ILLUSTRATION ON OPPOSITE PAGE].—*Height, 8¼ inches.*

	113	111	110
Top	114	112	109

113. MEISSEN DECORATED PORCELAIN FIGURE

XIX CENTURY

Figure of Amor, with pink shawl draped around body and a quiver hung over his shoulder. On circular marbleized base. (*Property of a New York Lady*). [SEE ILLUSTRATION].—*Height, 8¾ inches.*

114. MEISSEN DECORATED PORCELAIN FIGURE

XIX CENTURY

Seated Amor squeezing two hearts in a clamp. (*Property of a New York Lady*). (chipped). [SEE ILLUSTRATION].—*Height, 8⅝ inches.*

115

115. MEISSEN DECORATED PORCELAIN GROUP

XIX CENTURY

Allegorical group. Six figures on different levels of a rocky garden grouped around a tall tree. At top a gentleman holding out a watch towards a girl seated spinning; below them a couple, the man holding a bird and the girl an empty cage; on the other side a barefoot boy coming to wake a sleeping girl. All in rococo attire, the women in striped underskirts and colored bodices, the men in costumes of similar colors. On a circular base with molded geometrical design. (imperfect). (*Property of a New York Lady*). [SEE ILLUSTRATION]. —*Height; 17 inches.*

22

117   116

116. MEISSEN DECORATED PORCELAIN GROUP

XIX CENTURY

Allegorical group representing Gardening. Six figures on different
levels of a rocky garden; at top a gentleman with a basket of flowers
holding out a rose to a girl with her apron full of blossoms and a
basket on her head; below them a young boy with a watering pot
and a girl raking; and behind them a little girl seated holding a
flower pot and a man resting his foot on a spade; all dressed in rococo
attire, the women in striped underskirts and colored bodices, the
men in costumes of similar colors. On a circular base with a molded
geometrical ornament. (chipped and repaired). (*Property of a New
York Lady*). [SEE ILLUSTRATION].—*Height, 12 inches.*

117. MEISSEN DECORATED PORCELAIN GROUP

XIX CENTURY

Group of two boys and two girls wearing striped skirts and trousers,
blue and rose frocks and waists, laced bodices and black hats, holding
flowers, fruits, and gardening tools in their hands; the four figures
are posed on rocailles, brackets and a tree trunk on a circular stepped
base garlanded with rose drapery and an oak leaf festoon. (chipped).
(*Property of a New York Lady*). [SEE ILLUSTRATION].—*Height,
10½ inches.*

118. MEISSEN DECORATED PORCELAIN FIGURE

XVIII CENTURY

Reclining sheep with black and brown spots on white fleece. (legs repaired). (*New York Private Collector*).—*Length, 2⅛ inches.*

119. MEISSEN DECORATED PORCELAIN FIGURE

XIX CENTURY

Amor with hands and wings bound behind him. Amor seated on a rock with light blue drapery over his knees. On a circular marbleized base. (*Property of a New York Lady*). (chipped).—*Height, 6¾ inches.*

120. MEISSEN DECORATED PORCELAIN DOG   XVIII CENTURY

Seated figure with ribbon tied around neck, seated on a yellow pad. (imperfect). (*Property of a New York Lady*).—*Height, 4¾ inches.*

121. MEISSEN DECORATED PORCELAIN DOG   XVIII CENTURY

Barking dog on grassy base. (tail and ears restored). (*New York Private Collector*).—*Length, 2½ inches.*

122. MEISSEN DECORATED PORCELAIN GROUP

Representing the Rape of Proserpina. Neptune carrying Proserpina on his shoulder. On rocaille base. (imperfect) (*New York Private Collector*).—*Height, 10 inches.*

123. MEISSEN DECORATED PORCELAIN GROUP

Representing the Autumn. Young girl and boy in rococo attire; she holds basket with grapes, and he holds a bottle of wine and grapes; on a rocaille base. (*New York Private Collector*).—*Height, 6¼ inches.*

124. TWELVE MEISSEN DECORATED BUTTONS

XVIII CENTURY

Seven circular and five oval buttons, decorated with flower bouquets in colors. (*New York Private Collector*).

125. MEISSEN DECORATED PORCELAIN GROUP

XIX CENTURY

Group of three children. A young girl with her apron full of flowers holding out a rose to a boy, who is looking affectionately up to her; beside them a young boy is busy carving a doll which is rested on a sleigh in front of him. All in rococo costumes. On a gilt rocaille base. (chipped). (*Property of a New York Lady*). [SEE ILLUSTRATION ON OPPOSITE PAGE].—*Height, 7⅜ inches.*

24

	128	127	129
Top	126	125	126

126. PAIR MEISSEN DECORATED PORCELAIN GROUPS

XIX CENTURY

A girl with a ram and a boy with a goat, decking them with grapevine festoons; girl wearing a skirt with floral decoration and an orchid bodice, with basket of fruit hung around her shoulder; the boy is dressed in purple trousers and orchid frock. On oval base with gilt and molded geometrical design. (chipped). (*Property of a New York Lady*). [SEE ILLUSTRATION].—*Height, 6 inches.*

127. MEISSEN DECORATED PORCELAIN GROUP

XIX CENTURY

Allegorical group representing War. Two *puttis*, one seated, wearing helmet, resting his right hand on a bundle of *fasces*, the other standing, playing a drum, leaning against armor. On gilt rocaille base. (imperfect). (*Property of a New York Lady*). [SEE ILLUSTRATION]. —*Height, 5⅞ inches.*

25

128. MEISSEN DECORATED PORCELAIN GROUP

XIX CENTURY

90

Allegorical group representing Painting. Two *puttis* sitting in front of an easel glancing at a drawing. Grassy rocaille base enriched with molded busts of child and woman. (imperfect). (*Property of a New York Lady*). [SEE ILLUSTRATION ON PRECEDING PAGE].—*Length, 6¼ inches.*

129. MEISSEN DECORATED PORCELAIN GROUP

XIX CENTURY

75

Allegorical group representing Music. Two seated *puttis* with lyre between them; one holding a sheet of music on his lap and a scroll in his left hand, the other playing a flute; a tambourine beside them. On gilt rocaille base. (imperfect). (*Property of a New York Lady*). [SEE ILLUSTRATION ON PRECEDING PAGE].—*Length, 6½ inches.*

130. THIME DECORATED PORCELAIN FIGURE

XIX CENTURY

45

Standing figure of a girl, dressed in white blouse and blue bodice, striped skirt with flower decoration and bonnet, holding basket with flowers under her arm and roses in each hand. On rocaille base. (*Property of a New York Lady*). [SEE ILLUSTRATION ON OPPOSITE PAGE].—*Height, 5½ inches.*

131. PAIR MEISSEN DECORATED PORCELAIN FIGURES

XIX CENTURY

108

Standing figures of fiddler and flutist; one wearing tricorn, the other a high hat, both dressed in striped trousers and orchid color frock; leaning against tree trunks. On grassy rocaille bases. (chipped). (*Property of a New York Lady*). [SEE ILLUSTRATION ON OPPOSITE PAGE].—*Height, 5½ inches.*

132. MEISSEN DECORATED PORCELAIN FIGURE

XIX CENTURY

60

Standing girl dressed in rose hoop skirt and lace-trimmed bodice and striped underskirt with floral decoration, holding basket with flowers in her right hand and a rose in her left hand. On a rocaille base. (*Property of a New York Lady*). [SEE ILLUSTRATION ON OPPOSITE PAGE].—*Height, 5¾ inches.*

133. MEISSEN DECORATED PORCELAIN FIGURE

XIX CENTURY

45

Seated figure of a lady playing flute, dressed in rose robe with flower decoration. On grassy base. (chipped). (*Property of a New York Lady*). [SEE ILLUSTRATION ON OPPOSITE PAGE].—*Height, 5 inches.*

	131		134 .		133
Top	130		132		131

134. MEISSEN DECORATED PORCELAIN FIGURE

XIX CENTURY

Standing figure of a pastry baker; wearing a pink frock, blue striped trousers and white apron and cap; presenting a piece of pastry and a candy box on a rushed tray. On a rocaille base. (*Property of a New York Lady*). [SEE ILLUSTRATION].—*Height, 5 inches.*

135. PAIR MEISSEN DECORATED PORCELAIN PLATES

XIX CENTURY

Scalloped gilt edge, border pierced in geometrical design, decorated at center with finely painted pictures of mounted Turkish warriors. (*New York Private Collector*).—*Diameter, 9½ inches.*

27

136. PAIR MEISSEN DECORATED VASES   XIX CENTURY

Beaker-shaped with flaring mouth, having blue and gold border at top and bottom and flower bouquets around periphery. (*New York Private Collector*).—*Height, 5½ inches.*

137. MEISSEN DECORATED PORCELAIN CUP AND SAUCER

XVIII CENTURY

Bell-shaped with branch handle, molded basket-weave and swirled body, decorated with flower sprays in colors. (*New York Private Collector*).

138. MEISSEN DECORATED PORCELAIN PLATTER

Circa 1850

Square plate having finely molded edge with molded and gilt rocailles, scroll ornaments and shells at corners, centering flower bouquet in bright colors. (*New York Private Collector*).—15¾ *inches square.*

139. MEISSEN MINIATURE ON PORCELAIN   XVIII CENTURY

Portrait of a young lady wearing flowers in her high, powdered hair-dress, dressed in lace-trimmed blue bodice. Etched gold framing. In contemporary silvered frame. (*New York Private Collector*).— *Height, 2 inches.*

140. MEISSEN DECORATED PORCELAIN PLATE

XVIII CENTURY

Circular with scalloped edge, decorated with flower bouquets in molded and gilt cartouches at border. Centering view of the City of Utrecht in a rocaille cartouche. Inscription under foot: "De Stad Utrecht van het Paarden Veldtezien." (*New York Private Collector*). —*Diameter, 9½ inches.*

NOTE: Pieces of this set are in Victoria and Albert Museum, London; in Metropolitan Museum, New York, and in the possession of Queen Wilhelmina of Holland.

141. MEISSEN DECORATED PORCELAIN SAUCER

XVIII CENTURY

Similar to the preceding. Depicting: "Het Huise Groenestein." (*New York Private Collector*).—*Diameter, 6 inches.*

142. MEISSEN DECORATED SMALL CIRCULAR DISH

XVIII CENTURY

Similar to the preceding. Depicting: "Het Castel de Heukelum." (*New York Private Collector*).—*Diameter, 8 inches.*

143. MEISSEN DECORATED PORCELAIN NEEDLE BOX
XVIII CENTURY
Cylindrical box decorated with finely painted fruits and flowers in colors on white ground, gilt copper mounting. (*New York Private Collector*).—*Length, 5½ inches.*

144. MEISSEN DECORATED PORCELAIN NEEDLE BOX
XVIII CENTURY
Finely molded and decorated in shape of a fish, mounted in gilt copper. (*New York Private Collector*).—*Length, 5⅜ inches.*

145. MEISSEN DECORATED PORCELAIN CUP AND SAUCER
XVIII CENTURY
Bell-shaped with loop scroll handle, molded ribbed body, decorated with Indian flower pattern in purple and gold. (*New York Private Collector*).

146. PAIR MEISSEN DECORATED PORCELAIN CUPS AND SAUCERS
XIX CENTURY
Egg-shaped on tripart paw feet, twisted snake handle, decorated with figural scenes and flowers in gold medallions on rose ground. (*New York Private Collector*).

147. MEISSEN DECORATED PORCELAIN COMPOTE
XIX CENTURY
Deep basket on tripod pierced scroll foot; finely molded and painted branches of roses, leaves and buds arranged around basket and foot; sprays of flowers decoration on the interior of the basket. (chipped). (*Property of a New York Lady*).—*Diameter, 7½ inches.*

148. MEISSEN DECORATED PORCELAIN FIGURE
XVIII CENTURY
Standing figure of shepherdess with flowers in her apron, reclining sheep beside her, on circular base with molded flowers. (repaired). (*New York Private Collector*). [SEE ILLUSTRATION ON FOLLOWING PAGE].—*Height, 6½ inches.*

149. MEISSEN DECORATED PORCELAIN FIGURE
XVIII CENTURY
Standing figure of a nymph with a *putti* beside her. On irregular base having molded flowers. (repaired and chipped). (*New York Private Collector*). [SEE ILLUSTRATION ON FOLLOWING PAGE],—*Height, 5⅛ inches.*

150. PAIR MEISSEN DECORATED PORCELAIN TEA CADDIES
XVIII CENTURY
Flattened oblong with arched top and cover, decorated with landscapes of ruins and shore scenes, flower sprays and fruits at shoulder and top. (covers imperfect). (*New York Private Collector*). [SEE ILLUSTRATION ON FOLLOWING PAGE].—*Height, 4½ inches.*

	150		151		150
Top	148.		153		149

151. MEISSEN DECORATED PORCELAIN COVERED CUP AND
SAUCER   *Circa* 1780
Flattened globular with twisted branch handles, domed cover, laurel
ring finial. Decorated with town views in medallions and gold on
royal blue marbleized ground. (*New York Private Collector*). [SEE
ILLUSTRATION].

152. MEISSEN BLUE AND WHITE ONION PATTERN COFFEE
SET
Comprising twelve cups, twelve saucers, twelve cake plates with
pierced border, honey jar, drip coffee maker and milkpot. (39 pieces).
(*New York Private Collector*).

30

104   154   155

153. NYMPHENBURG DECORATED PORCELAIN DOG

XVIII CENTURY

Standing figure of a white hound with dark spots, on oblong base.
(tail restored). (*New York Private Collector*). [SEE ILLUSTRATION
ON OPPOSITE PAGE].—*Length, 7½ inches.*

154. HOECHST DECORATED PORCELAIN GROUP

Johann Peter Melchior, XVIII CENTURY

Allegorical group representing History. Four *putti* grouped on different levels of the rock base; one seated at center resting his arm
on a book while another holds up flowers behind him; *putto* at right
taking flowers from filled cornucopia, at left holding a panel with
inscription: "Geschichte." A globe, a palette, books and instruments arranged at the base. (repaired). (*Property of a New York
Lady*). [SEE ILLUSTRATION].—*Height, 9¼ inches.*

NOTE: Johann Peter Melchior, one of the most famous modelers,
was born in 1742 and worked at the Hoechst factory until 1778 at
which time he went, in the same capacity, to Frankenthal where he
remained for three years. Afterwards he worked for the Nymphenburg factory where he remained until his death in 1825.

155. FRANKENTHAL DECORATED PORCELAIN GROUP

Johann Peter Melchior, Frankenthal, 1779

Mythological group, representing Venus binding Amor's eyes. Venus
with open classical hairdress and white shawl draped around her
body standing beside Amor on shell; a *putto* with a quiver in his
left hand and arrow in his right hand seated by waterweeds in the
back. On a rocky base. (*Property of a New York Lady*). [SEE
ILLUSTRATION].—*Height, 11½ inches.*

31

156

156. CAPO DI MONTE DECORATED PORCELAIN TABLE
DECORATION
Six allegorical figures of women in richly draped gilt dresses in various poses, On quadrangular bases with ram's heads at corners and hoof feet. (*Property of a New York Lady*). [SEE ILLUSTRATION].—
Height, 10¼ inches.

157. THREE COPENHAGEN DECORATED PORCELAIN BIRDS
Figures of sparrows, decorated in colors. (one chipped). (*New York Private Collector*).—*Heights, from 1¾ to 2⅜ inches.*

158. VIENNESE DECORATED PORCELAIN DEMI-TASSE SET
ON BRONZE TRAY
One cup, two saucers, coffee pot and sugar bowl with figural and *putti* decoration in panels on green ground; on an oblong gilt bronze tray. (*New York Private Collector*).

32

159. THIME DECORATED PORCELAIN VASE
Slender ovoid with wide flaring neck, decorated with tooled gold flowers and portrait of a young girl in colors in tooled gold medallion on a fluctuating blue ground. (*New York Private Collector*).— *Height, 9¼ inches.*

160. CONTINENTAL DECORATED PORCELAIN CHOCOLATE SET
Comprising two cups and saucers, chocolate pot and covered sugar bowl, with figural decoration in tooled gold panels, on an iridescent green ground. (chipped). (6 pieces). (*New York Private Collector*).

161. ZURICH DECORATED PORCELAIN MINIATURE FIGURE
XVIII CENTURY
Standing figure of a peasant woman carrying baskets with grapes on her back and in her arms. On circular base. (*New York Private Collector*).—*Height, 2½ inches.*

162. PAIR CAPO DI MONTE DECORATED PORCELAIN MINIATURE VASES
XVIII CENTURY
Ovoid with flaring neck, circular foot, dolphin handles, molded in shell design at shoulder and base. Decorated with spray of flowers in colors. (*New York Private Collector*).—*Height, 3½ inches.*

163. PAIR ROYAL BERLIN DECORATED PORCELAIN FIGURES
Boy and girl disguised as Zeus and Athena; both wearing crown and mantle holding sceptre in their hands. On square base. (one imperfect). (*Property of a New York Lady*).—*Height, 4½ inches.*

164. TWO ROYAL BERLIN DECORATED PORCELAIN FIGURES
Standing figure of a boy representing Winter; wearing green jacket, striped yellow trousers and fur hat; he is hiding his hand in his jacket and carries skates on his arm. On square base. The other, standing boy, playing a flute and with bird cage and a bird in his left hand. (one chipped). (*Property of a New York Lady*).—*Heights, 5¼ and 6¼ inches.*

165. LUDWIGSBURG DECORATED PORCELAIN GROUP
XVIII CENTURY
A boy and a peasant girl; she is seated on a sheaf of wheat holding bowl on her lap and spoon in her hand; the boy sitting on tree trunk with a bottle of wine rested on his knee and a glass in his left hand; on oblong base. (repaired). (*Property of a New York Lady*).— *Height, 4½ inches.*

33

167
Top 166

166. LUDWIGSBURG DECORATED PORCELAIN GROUP

XVIII CENTURY

Allegorical group representing Autumn. A nude couple reclining on a striped drapery; the woman pressing grapes into a goblet held by the man, who looks up at her; he holds a wine jar in his left hand; basket of grapes posed behind the woman. On a rocky base enriched with plants. (repaired). (*Property of a New York Lady*). [SEE ILLUSTRATION].—*Length, 11¾ inches.*

34

167. LUDWIGSBURG DECORATED PORCELAIN GROUP
XVIII CENTURY

A naked nymph reclining on a striped drapery, one arm around the satyr's head who is seated behind her; a baby satyr lying across her lap. On rocky base enriched with molded fruits. (*Property of a New York Lady*). [SEE ILLUSTRATION ON OPPOSITE PAGE].—*Length, 10¼ inches.*
En suite with the preceding.

168. ROYAL BERLIN DECORATED TABLE CENTER

Large, deep bowl, pierced in geometrical design, resting on a metal base, supported by three sphinxes on a curved trilateral stepped base; invested with white glaze. (*Property of a New York Lady*).— *Diameter, 16 inches.*

169. ROSENTHAL DECORATED PORCELAIN GROUP

Lady and harlequin; a lady in hoop skirt and rose bodice dancing with a harlequin with mask and cap and bells. On a rocaille base. (*New York Private Collector*).—*Height, 6 inches.*

170. MEISSEN DECORATED PORCELAIN FRUIT BOWL

Oblong with molded and gilt rocailles and scroll ornaments at edge and bottom, on a cobalt blue ground. (*New York Private Collector*). —*Length, 11½ inches.*

DECORATIONS

GLASS, PORCELAINS, MANTEL GARNITURES

171. SEVEN BACCARAT ROSE PRESSED GLASS COMPOTES

One sherbet and six small compotes with swirled body and foot and scalloped edge.—*Diameters, 5¼ to 6 inches.*

172. FOUR BACCARAT ROSE PRESSED GLASS COMPOTES

Similar to the preceding.—Diameters, 3¼ to 5¼ inches.

173. SEVEN BACCARAT ROSE PRESSED GLASS COMPOTES

Similar to the preceding.—Diameters, 5½ to 7 inches.

174. THREE BACCARAT ROSE PRESSED GLASS COMPOTES

Similar to the preceding.—Diameters, 5½ to 6 inches.

175. FOUR BACCARAT ROSE PRESSED GLASS COMPOTES

Similar to the preceding.—Diameters, 5½ to 6¼ inches.

176. FOUR CLEAR GLASS BOTTLES

Two quadrangular, cut with diamond and button design; one cylindrical cut in panels with knopped stopper and one of frosted glass with metal top.—*Heights, 4¾ to 6½ inches.*

35

177. THREE CLEAR GLASS DECANTERS   XVIII CENTURY
Pair of canted tapering cylindrical decanters with flaring neck and
knopped stoppers, decorated with flowers and scroll ornaments in
gold, and a small bottle with diamond cut. (one chipped).

178. TWO MILK WHITE BLOWN GLASS VASES
A globular vase with flaring fluted neck and molded rose decoration;
the other tapering cylindrical with knopped shaft on circular base
with floral decoration in colors.—*Heights, 7 and 7¾ inches.*

179. THREE OVERLAY GLASS DECANTERS
Globular with high cylindrical neck having red overlay, decorated
with the Persian lion and flowers in red overlay, outlined in gold.—
Height, 11¾ inches.

180. FOUR CLEAR GLASS BOWLS AND UNDER-DISHES
Deep footed bowls cut in panels and four plates with scalloped edge
and star cut at bottom.. (8 pieces).

181. THREE CLEAR GLASS OBJECTS
Two relish dishes cut in diamond and button design and an oblong
tray with scalloped edge.

182. CLEAR GLASS COVERED MUG AND UNDER-DISH
Tapering cylindrical mug with loop handle, domed cover, knob finial
on circular under-dish, etched with floral and scroll ornaments.
(chipped).—*Height, 9¾ inches.*

183. CLEAR GLASS BONBONNIERE
Large cut glass bonbonniere with bull's-eye, leaf and diamond pattern,
with under-dish etched in a floral design.

184. IMPERIAL RUSSIAN DECORATED PORCELAIN MUG
AND SAUCER
Cylindrical mug with scroll loop handle, domed cover and knob finial,
on circular scalloped saucer. Decoration of flowers on rose and white
ground.

185. THREE ORIENTAL LOWESTOFT DECORATED
PORCELAIN PLATES   *Circa* 1820
Deep circular plate decorated with lattice work and flower festoons
at border and flower bouquet at center. (one chipped).—*Diameter,*
10½ inches.

186. THREE ORIENTAL LOWESTOFT DECORATED
PORCELAIN PLATES   *Circa* 1820
One decorated with flowers in panels and gold stars on blue ground
at border, centering flower bouquet; the second with diaper design,
flowers and stars on blue ground at border and flower bouquet at
center; the third having border of geometrical design, small flower
sprays with center of sun design.—*Diameters, 9 to 10½ inches.*

187. TWO BOHEMIAN DECORATED PORCELAIN PLATES
Circular plates decorated with flowers in blue and gold at border
centering portrait of a Persian Shah in colors in a gold medallion.—
Diameter, 9 inches.

188. TWO FRENCH DECORATED PORCELAIN VASES
Flattened bell-shaped with molded handles, with floral decoration in
gold.—*Heights, 5 and 6 inches.*

189. THREE ORIENTAL LOWESTOFT OBJECTS   XVIII CENTURY
A deep bowl with floral and bird decoration in *rouge de fer* and gold,
and two saucers, one decorated with flowers in colors and the other
with flowers and cartouches in blue and gold on white ground.

190. TWO BOHEMIAN DECORATED PORCELAIN PLATES
Deep circular plates allover decorated with flower and leaf design in
cobalt blue and gold on white ground.—*Diameter, 10⅞ inches.*

191. CHINESE DECORATED PORCELAIN PLATE
Deep circular plate with scalloped edge and decorated in relief with
tiger in landscape.—*Diameter, 11 inches.*

192. PAIR CHINESE DECORATED PORCELAIN BOWLS
Deep bowls, decorated wiht landscapes and figures in colors on white
ground.—*Diameter, 6 inches.*

193. CHINESE BLUE AND WHITE DECORATED PORCELAIN
PLATE
Allover decorated with flowers and leaves in blue on white ground.—
Diameter, 15¼ inches.

194. TWELVE MINTON DECORATED PORCELAIN FISH
PLATES   *Tiffany & Co.*
Circular plate with gilt edge decorated with grapevine design and
festoons in tooled gold on apple green ground at border, centering
under-water scene, with fish in colors, in a tooled gold hexagonal
medallion. (*New York Private Collector*).—*Diameter, 9 inches.*

37

195. TWO DECORATED ROYAL DOULTON PORCELAIN
VASES
One globular with high tapering neck, decorated with scenes of
children, and molded floral decoration in gold at neck; the other,
bottle shaped with funnel neck and dragon handle, floral decoration
in colors on a cream rough ground. (chipped). (*New York Private
Collector*).—*Heights, 10 and 11 inches.*

196. PAIR SEVRES DECORATED PORCELAIN VASES
MOUNTED IN BRONZE
Tapering cylindrical vases with domed covers, decorated with figural
scenes and flower bouquets in gold medallion on royal blue ground.
Mounted at top and bottom in pierced and chased bronze with ram's-
head and beaded loose handle. (cover repaired). (*New York Private
Collector*).—*Height, 16 inches.*

197. DECORATED PORCELAIN VASE MOUNTED AS LAMP
Slender ovoid, short neck, circular foot and ring handles, decorated
with molded ornaments in gold on shoulder and base, and flower
decoration in colors and gold around body. Fitted for electricity.
(*New York Private Collector*).—*Height, 30 inches.*

198. PAIR CHINESE DECORATED PORCELAIN PLATES
CH'IEN LUNG
Circular plate decorated with flowers and fruit branches in *rouge de
fer*, blue and gold. (*New York Private Collector*).—*Diameter, 8¾
inches.*
NOTE: These plates were formerly in the Royal Saxonian Collection
Joanneum at Dresden. Each bears the incised Joanneum mark 146
and cross under foot.

199. PAIR SEVRES DECORATED PORCELAIN VASES
Urn-shaped with funnel neck and flaring lip on circular stepped base,
having black and gold rings around neck and foot, invested with
brown glaze.—*Height, 15 inches.*

200. PAIR ORIENTAL DECORATED PORCELAIN VASES
Slender ovoid with quadrangular neck and overlapping lip. Decorated
with figural scenes and landscapes in tooled gold and enamel color
medallions, on a crackled ground.—*Height, 17¼ inches.*

201. PAIR DECORATED PORCELAIN VASES AND
JARDINIERE MOUNTED IN BRONZE
Ovoid vase and an oval jardiniere all on circular bases, decorated
with figural scenes in tooled gold medallions, having bronze handles,
bases and edging. (imperfect). (*New York Private Collector*).—
Heights, from 5 to 7¼ inches.

202. BRONZE AND CRYSTAL GIRANDOLES
Shaft of circular mirror flanked by knopped candleholder and circular drip cup hung with prisms. On square mirror base and four paw feet. Fitted for electricity. (*New York Private Collector*).—*Height, 11 inches.*

203. TWO SETS OF CANTON ENAMEL BOXES
Each set composed of three cylindrical boxes with circular cover decorated with figural scenes in panels and flowers and ornaments on yellow and green ground. (*New York Private Collector*).—*Diameter, 3⅞ inches.*

204. CHINESE WHITE GLAZED PORCELAIN INCENSE BURNER
Globular with elephant head handles, tripart stump mascaron feet; invested with cream crackled glaze. Pierced teakwood cover with carved soapstone Deity as finial. (*New York Private Collector*).—*Diameter, 15 inches.*
From Edward I. Farmer, Inc., New York

205. THREE CERAMIC OBJECTS
Bohemian decorated porcelain creamer, with floral and scroll ornament decoration in panels on blue ground; a Viennese miniature cup and saucer with figural scene at front, on rose ground, gilt interior and handle; and a Gmunden inkwell, quadrangular with pierced sides in a floral design. (repaired). (*New York Private Collector*).

206. TWO HISPANO MORESQUE POTTERY PLATES
XVII CENTURY
Deep circular plates, one decorated with stylized flowers in blue and scroll ornaments in copper lustre; the other, with stylized birds and flowers in copper lustre. (both repaired). (*New York Private Collector*).—*Diameters, 12 and 13 inches.*

207. A LEAD AND A BRONZE PLAQUE
Circular lead plaque depicting Mozart and a bronze plaque showing head of Bacchus. (*New York Private Collector*).—*Diameters, 6 and 7 inches.*

208. TWO DECORATED POTTERY VASES
One tapering clindrical, the other ovoid with gilt loop handle decorated with flowers in colors and gold on cream crackled ground. (*New York Private Collector*).—*Heights, 5¾ and 6¾ inches.*

209. BRONZE FIGURE OF MERCURY
After the original by Giovanni da Bologna; on circular marble base, enriched with bronze relief of *putti* with musical instruments. (*New York Private Collector*).—*Height, 36 inches.*

210. BRONZE FIGURE OF MOSES
After the original by Michelangelo Buanarotti. (*New York Private Collector*).—*Height, 14½ inches.*

211. VICTORIAN MARBLE AND BRONZE MANTEL. GARNITURE
Oblong clock case on stepped base with curved bronze feet and bronze lion-head ring handles, surmounted by a marble vase with bronze mountings. Fitted with eight-day striking movement. Pair of candelabra with scroll bronze arms and center light on incurved cylindrical marble base and bronze scroll feet. (*New York Private Collector*).—*Height, 13½ inches.*

212. VICTORIAN GILDED BRONZE MANTEL GARNITURE
High oblong clock case with arched top supported by columns, surmounted by architectural cresting with vase finial; on oblong outset pediment base with scroll and quadrangular feet. Fitted with eight-day striking movement. Pair candelabra with four scroll arms emanating from vase-shaped shaft on quadrangular domed pediment base with scroll feet. Fitted for electricity. (*New York Private Collector*).—*Height, 26½ inches.*

213. VICTORIAN BRONZE MANTEL GARNITURE
High oblong clock case with arched top, surmounted by laurel wreath encircling gilt medallion; case is flanked by torchères with gilt mascarons and rests on oblong stepped base with outset corners and rounded sides. Fitted with eight-day striking movement. Pair of candelabra with two scroll arms and center light on tapering fluted knopped shaft and stepped oblong base with outset corners. (*New York Private Collector*).—*Heights, 13¾ and 15½ inches.*

214. PRAGUE DECORATED PORCELAIN DESSERT SET
Comprising six plates and a compote, decorated with fruits in colors on white ground and gilt edge. (*New York Private Collector*).

END OF SALE

CPSIA information can be obtained
at www.ICGtesting.com
Printed in the USA
BVHW032125251122
652781BV00004B/158